GETTING THE BEST
FROM YOUR
MICROWAVE

Consultant Editor:
Valerie Ferguson

southwater

Contents

Introduction

The microwave oven has brought the art of cooking into the twenty-first century. Not only does it cook food more rapidly than a conventional oven, but it does it superbly well. Colour, flavour and texture are retained and, because cooking times are precise, dried-out dishes are things of the past. As additional cooking liquid is minimal, fewer nutrients are lost during cooking. Food can be cooked with the minimum of attention in the knowledge that it will be appetizing and cooked to exactly the right degree.

As cooking times may be reduced by up to 75 per cent, the microwave uses less energy and so cuts costs. Finally, because you can cook and serve in the same container, there is less washing-up.

Almost anything, from the simple baked potato to dinner party dishes, can be cooked in the microwave, and some types of food are particularly well suited to it. Fish and seafood are ideal, as their delicate texture and flavour are preserved. Vegetables can be cooked to tender-crisp perfection with only the minimal amount of water. Cooking rice and pasta in the microwave saves little time, but it does guarantee superb results and no sticky pans to wash.

All About Microwaves

Understanding how this form of energy works will help you to use it efficiently and with maximum benefit.

What are Microwaves?

Microwaves are electro-magnetic waves that are reflected by some materials, such as metal, pass through some, such as glass, and are absorbed by some, such as water.

How they Work

Household electricity is converted into microwaves by a magnetron vacuum tube inside the microwave oven and the microwaves are directed into the oven cavity and stirred by a fan for even distribution. The metal lining inside the base and walls of the oven contain the microwaves within the cavity and the doors and frames of all models are fitted with special safety seals so that microwaves do not escape.

Speedy Cooking

Microwaves cook differently from conventional methods. They are absorbed by the moisture in food, causing the food molecules to vibrate rapidly – millions of times per second. This produces intense heat, which cooks the food very fast, while the container remains cool and can therefore be rotated or moved without needing oven gloves. (Dishes and plates must be microwaveproof.)

Above: There is a wide range of foods that can be cooked quickly and with less effort and energy use in a microwave.

FOOD FACTS

The factors that affect microwave cooking differ from those that apply to conventional methods.

Starting Temperature

Foods that are cooked from room temperature will take less time to cook than frozen or chilled foods. The cooking times given in this book are based on starting temperatures at which foods are normally stored.

Density

The denser the food, the longer it takes to cook. Potatoes, for example take longer than sponge cakes. Similarly, a dense mass of food, such as a whole cauliflower, takes longer than the same quantity divided into pieces and spread out.

Composition

Foods that are high in fats and sugars absorb microwave energy more readily than those that are high in liquids, and so cook faster. They also reach higher temperatures. Equally, foods that are low in moisture, such as cakes, cook faster than those with a high water content, such as vegetables.

Quantity

The more food you put in the microwave, the longer it takes to cook. If you double the given amount, the cooking time will increase by about half as much again.

Size and Shape

Smaller pieces of food cook more quickly than larger ones and uniformly shaped pieces cook more evenly than irregular ones. If unevenly shaped food cannot be cut into regular shapes – chicken drumsticks, for example – arrange it with the thinner part towards the centre of the dish. The thicker sections will receive most energy and cook quickly. Round and ring shapes cook more evenly than square, oval or rectangular ones. You can shield the corners of dishes with small pieces of smooth foil to prevent charring.

Above: Vegetables and fruit cooked in the microwave keep their colour, flavour, texture and a high proportion of their vitamin content.

Dishes & Utensils

The microwave oven enables you to use a wider range of equipment than for conventional cooking.

Special Equipment

There are many specialist innovations in microwave cookware. Several ranges manufactured from polythene, polystyrene and thermoplastics are widely available and come in a comprehensive range of sizes and shapes. A browning dish is a useful extra. Made of a glass ceramic substance with a coating that absorbs microwave energy, the dish is preheated in the microwave until the base coating changes colour – usually for about 8 minutes on HIGH, but always follow the manufacturer's instructions. Browning dishes have many applications: they are useful for burgers, chops, sausages and steaks and can also be used to "fry" eggs and sandwiches and to brown vegetables.

Above: There are now a wide range of cookware made especially for the different functions of a microwave.

Cotton & Linen

Napkins are ideal for short warming, such as reheating rolls before serving. Avoid synthetic fibres and fabrics containing a proportion of them, as they will be damaged.

Paper

Napkins, kitchen paper, paper cups, cartons, paper freezer wrap and the paper pulp board often used for supermarket packaging are all suitable when thawing, reheating or for very short cooking and for foods with a low fat, sugar or water content. Avoid wax-coated cups and plates.

Above: Many items of domestic cookware can be used and often the same container can go from oven to table for serving.

suitable for roasting or boil-in-the-bag cooking work well. Pierce a bag or film before cooking to allow steam to escape and take extra care when opening plastic bags to avoid being scalded. Replace any metal ties with elastic or string. Do not use thin polythene bags, as they will not withstand the heat of the food, although thicker storage or freezer bags are acceptable.

Above: Avoid using any of these items in the microwave oven.

Glass, Pottery & China

Ovenproof and plain glass, pottery and china are all suitable. Check that containers do not have a metallic trim, screws or handles. Ovenproof glass and glass ceramic dishes are ideal, as they can go from freezer to microwave and vice versa.

Wooden & Wicker

These may be used for short periods of reheating, but wood or wicker will tend to dry out, crack or char.

Plastics

Thermoplastic materials are microwave-proof, but other plastics are likely to melt or distort, especially if used for cooking foods with a high fat or sugar content. Dishwasher-safe plastic is a good indication of suitability for the microwave. Plastic or clear film for use in the microwave and items such as bags

Out of Bounds

Metal in any form is unsuitable for use in the microwave oven, except for small pieces of smooth foil used for shielding vulnerable areas of food or dishes. This prohibition includes foil dishes, china with a metal design, metal skewers and even paper-coated metal ties for plastic bags. Do not use unglazed earthenware or leaded glass. Avoid mugs and cups with glued-on handles, as these can loosen and so could cause a scald.

Techniques

Your success in using the microwave oven will be greater if you follow these simple rules every time you cook.

Preparing Ingredients

Cut ingredients into even-size pieces so that they cook at the same rate.

• Slice vegetables into slim strips.
• Large vegetables, such as swede or potatoes, can be cut into neat cubes to promote quick, even cooking.
• Slicing meat across the grain into thin pieces helps to tenderize it.

Scoring or Pricking Foods

Foods with tight skins or membranes, such as sausages, whole fish, jacket potatoes, egg yolks and apples must be lightly pricked or scored before cooking or they are liable to burst.

Stirring

In a microwave, stirring redistributes heat and cooked areas from the outside to the centre of a dish for even cooking. Precise stirring instructions are given in a recipe if it is important; if not, stirring halfway through cooking is usually sufficient to achieve a good result.

Rotating

If your microwave has a turntable, then this is not necessary. Otherwise, a quarter or half turn of the dish at regular intervals during cooking will ensure even results. This applies to food that cannot be either stirred or turned over.

Rearranging Food

Redistributing foods ensures even results. Move foods from the outside of the dish to the centre and vice versa.

• Rearrange foods cooked in a bag by gently shaking the bag from side to side.

Arranging Food

A careful arrangement of foods for microwave cooking can ensure that an ingredient is perfectly cooked.

• Try to cook foods of an even or similar size together and arrange them in a ring, leaving the centre empty.
• If foods are of an irregular shape, arrange them like spokes with the thicker sections to the outside of the dish. This will balance the cooking times of the thick and thin pieces.

• Arrange whole fish in pairs, head to tail, to form an even area that will cook uniformly.
• When reheating plated meals, ensure food is spread out evenly with thicker vegetables towards the edge so that they receive the most energy.

• Use special plastic microwave stacking rings when reheating more than one plated meal so that they all receive an equal amount of energy and reheat uniformly.
• Try to ensure an even depth of food. Otherwise, stir or rearrange ingredients to achieve this.
• Cakes cook best in a ring mould. If you don't have one, then there is a simple method you can use. Place a glass jar in a round microwaveproof dish and hold it in place while adding the mixture.

Turning Over

Many large or dense items of food, such as potatoes or chicken drumsticks, should be turned over about halfway through cooking to ensure good results.

Shielding

Some parts of foods are vulnerable to overcooking; protect them with small smooth strips of foil. It is important that the foil does not touch the oven walls. Place it on the food for about half the cooking time, secured with wooden cocktail sticks.

Check the manufacturer's handbook to ensure that this is permissible in your oven model.

> COOK'S TIP: Microwave-safe clear film is often the most practical choice of covering, allowing you to see what is happening in the dish. When folded back at one corner, the contents can be stirred during cooking without discarding it. Always remove the film carefully, starting at the side farthest away from you to avoid scalding your hands or bare forearms.

• Shield wing tips on poultry and the thinner tail-ends on ducks to prevent them from overcooking.
• Shield protruding bones, such as those you will find on a rack of lamb, to prevent scorching.
• Shield the narrow ends of joints of meat, such as at the end of a leg of lamb or pork.

• Protect fish heads and tails to prevent eyes from bursting and thin areas from overcooking. (If you prefer to serve fish without heads and tails, remove these before cooking.) Even though microwave cooking is a moist method, foods can dry out because of the speed with which moisture evaporates from them.

Covering & Wrapping

Problems of surfaces drying out, food splattering on the cavity walls and slower-than-optimum cooking times can all be eliminated by covering or wrapping foods. This locks in moisture, retains juices and speeds up cooking by trapping heat-retaining steam.

• Use double-strength plastic cooking bags, suitable for boiling ("boil-in-the-bag" or "cook-bags") or roasting bags for vegetables, meat and poultry. Replace metal ties with elastic bands.
• Some bags come with special, microwaveproof plastic clips.
• String can be used to tie bags loosely closed.

• Cover bowls tightly with microwave-safe clear film. Puncture the top to allow steam to escape during cooking.
• Turn back a small area of clear film to provide a vent. Take care when removing clear film, as it will trap scalding-hot steam even if vented.
• Greaseproof paper may be used to cover small bowls, for example. Secure it with a large elastic band.

• Use a tight-fitting, purpose-made lid or improvise by using a saucer or plate. Make sure that they are microwaveproof.

• Use kitchen paper to cover potatoes and bread, as it absorbs excess moisture.
• Covering bacon with kitchen paper prevents spattering and danger of nasty burns.
• Kitchen paper is good for making dried herbs and as a base on which to stand food.
• Dampened kitchen paper can be used for reheating and steaming pancakes and shellfish.

Removing Excess Cooking Juices

Any juices that seep from food will absorb microwave energy. If there is a great quantity and the cooking time is longer than about 5 minutes on HIGH, it is advisable to remove some liquid regularly during cooking, or the excess juices could prolong the cooking time. You might find this happens when cooking chicken, duck or turkey. Liquid can always be replaced towards the end of the cooking time if you find that the food starts to dry out too much.

Standing Times

Food continues to cook by conduction after the microwave energy has been turned off. As there is residual heat, it is important to err on the safe side and undercook rather than overcook food. There is no rescue package for overcooked food, but additional cooking time can be given if the dish is still inadequately cooked after observing the standing time.

Browning Foods

Foods cooked in the microwave do not readily brown. Try the following tips to encourage browning or disguise any pale results.

• Grill foods such as gratins and roasts before or after microwave cooking.

• Use a microwave browning dish for chops, steaks, fried eggs, toasted sandwiches, stir-fries and individual chicken portions.

• Buy or make a browning mix to coat foods – paprika, toasted breadcrumbs, crushed crisps, soy sauce, Worcestershire sauce and soup mixes all work well.

• Bacon browns readily, so it can be laid over poultry or roast meat.

• Baked items, such as cakes and biscuits, can be sprinkled or coated with toasted coconut, chocolate vermicelli, roughly chopped nuts, chopped glacé fruits, seeds, such as sunflower and poppy, and dark spices.

• Glaze ham, poultry or game with fruit preserve, particularly redcurrant jelly or citrus marmalade, before cooking, to add colour. Use a broad pastry brush for even coverage.

• Add icing to a pale cake or other baked items after cooking. Sprinkle it on just before serving.

COOK'S TIP: A bulb baster is a very useful kitchen gadget for removing excess liquid, particularly from awkwardly shaped food such as chicken, turkey or duck. It is widely available from all good kitchenware shops.

The Microwave & Freezer

Microwaves defrost food both quickly and efficiently. Almost all models have a DEFROST control or button to ensure optimum action.

Defrosting Tips

Refer to the manufacturer's handbook for a guide to defrosting times. Err on the side of safety by timing for too short a period, rather than too long.

• Follow standing times as foods will continue to thaw by conduction. Defrost until just icy.

• Open cartons and remove any metal lids, ties or fastenings before defrosting.

• Before defrosting, prick, slash or vent membranes and skins. Also, pierce clear film, pouches or similar wrappings.

• Never try to hurry the process.

• Transfer frozen foods in foil to a suitable dish for the microwave.

• Turn foods over during defrosting, halfway through the recommended time.

• If food cannot be turned, rotate it regularly for even defrosting.

• Flex and rotate pouches of food that cannot be broken up or stirred.

• Place cakes, rolls and pastry items on a double sheet of kitchen paper to absorb excess moisture.

• Break up blocks of frozen food with a fork during defrosting.

• Separate blocks of frozen meat items, such as hamburgers, as they defrost.

• Remove any juices or drips with a bulb baster or spoon.

• Defrost meat joints, whole birds and whole fish until icy, then leave to defrost completely at room temperature before cooking.

Freezer to Microwave Reminders

When freezing home-made food that will later be defrosted or cooked in the microwave, the following hints are worth noting.

• Freeze all cooked food in a microwaveproof container.

• Arrange cooked main courses on microwaveproof plates and freeze.

• Freeze soups, casseroles and hot pots in freezer bags that are also suitable for microwave defrosting.

Cook & Freeze in One Bag

1 Cook fruits such as apples and pears in a roasting bag or boilable bag.

2 When cooked, crush the fruit in the bag to make a purée and seal while still hot. As it cools it will form a vacuum pack that is ideal for freezing and ready for defrosting or reheating.

Making the Most of Your Microwave

These are just some of the cooking techniques that can be done in a matter of minutes. You will soon discover others that suit your style of cooking.

Peeling Peaches & Apricots

Place up to four peaches in a microwaveproof bowl with very little water. Cover and microwave on HIGH for 1–1½ minutes. Leave to stand for 5 minutes, then drain and peel.

Softening Butter

Microwave on HIGH for 5–10 seconds, then leave to stand for 5 minutes before using.

COOK'S TIP: Croûtons can be flavoured in a variety of ways to complement the dishes they garnish. A crushed garlic clove or a little dried oregano can be added to the butter for butter-crisp croûtons. Chopped fresh herbs, such as tarragon or parsley, should be tossed with the cooked croûtons. Grated Parmesan cheese or lemon rind can also be added to cooked croûtons.

To Make Croûtons

1 For dry, oil-free croûtons, dice 175 g/6 oz bread into cubes.

2 Place on kitchen paper on a large flat microwaveproof plate and microwave on HIGH for 3–4 minutes, stirring once every minute, until dry.

3 For butter-crisp croûtons, place 25 g/1 oz/2 tbsp butter in a microwaveproof dish and microwave on HIGH for 30 seconds to melt. Add 175 g/6 oz bread cubes and toss to coat. Microwave on HIGH for 3–4 minutes, stirring every minute, until crisp and brown. Freeze until needed (no need to defrost).

Peeling Tomatoes

Place up to six tomatoes in a ring on kitchen paper. Microwave on HIGH for 10–15 seconds. Leave to stand for 15 minutes, then peel.

To Dry Bread for Crumbs

1 Place a thick slice of bread on a microwaveproof plate and microwave on HIGH for 2½–3½ minutes.

2 When the bread is completely cool, grate it. Use at once or freeze until needed.

Garlic or Herb Bread

To serve four, cut a 115 g/4 oz French stick into diagonal slices about 4 cm/1½ in thick, almost to the base but not quite through. Spread garlic or herb butter between the slices and re-form the loaf. Wrap loosely in kitchen paper and microwave on HIGH for 1½ minutes. Serve at once.

Drying Herbs & Citrus Rinds

Position on a microwaveproof plate and microwave on HIGH until dry. Check at 1 minute intervals.

Proving Yeast Dough

Give a 900 g/2 lb piece of dough short bursts of microwave energy on HIGH for 5–10 seconds, with a 10 minute standing time between each burst. Repeat until the dough has risen to double its size.

Blanching Almonds

Place 250 ml/8 fl oz/1 cup water in a jug. Microwave on HIGH for 2½ minutes, until boiling. Add the almonds and microwave for 30 seconds. Drain and slip off the skins.

Toasting Nuts

Place the nuts in a browning dish and microwave on HIGH for 4–5 minutes, stirring each minute. For a lighter result, cook them in an ordinary microwaveproof dish. For desiccated coconut, spread 115 g/4 oz/1¼ cups on a plate and microwave on HIGH for 5–6 minutes, stirring every minute.

Squeezing Citrus Juice

To extract the maximum amount of juice from the fruit, prick the skins and then microwave on HIGH for about 5–10 seconds.

17

Defrosting Frozen Pastry

Place a 400 g/14 oz packet of pastry on a microwaveproof plate and microwave on DEFROST for 4–4½ minutes, turning over once. Leave to stand for 5 minutes before using.

Softening Jams & Spreads

Remove lids and any metal trims or transfer the jam to a microwaveproof dish. Microwave on HIGH for about 5–10 seconds per 450 g/1 lb.

Dissolving Gelatine

1 Sprinkle the gelatine over cold water and leave to stand in a cool place until spongy.

2 Microwave the gelatine on HIGH for 30 seconds, until clear and completely dissolved.

To Make Jelly

1 Break up a 130 g/4½ oz jelly tablet and place in a microwaveproof bowl or jug with 150 ml/¼ pint/⅔ cup water.

2 Microwave the jelly on HIGH for 2 minutes. Stir well to dissolve, then make up with cold water according to the packet instructions.

Clarifying Crystallized Honey

Remove the lid and any metal trims on the jar, and then microwave on HIGH for 1–2 minutes. Stir the honey well. To make clear honey more runny, microwave on DEFROST for 30–50 seconds.

Melting Chocolate

Break chocolate into pieces and place
in a microwaveproof bowl. Microwave
on HIGH, for about 1 minute per
25 g/1 oz.

Softening Ice Cream

Microwave about 1 litre/1¾ pints/
4 cups hard (not soft scoop) ice cream
on MEDIUM for 45–90 seconds.
Leave to stand for 1–2 minutes before
scooping into serving dishes.

Quick Soaking of
Dried Beans

Place the dried beans in a microwaveproof bowl and cover them with
boiling water. Cover and microwave
on HIGH for 5 minutes. Leave to
stand for 1½ hours, then drain, rinse
and cook the beans.

To Heat Milk for Drinks

Frothy hot milk for café au lait, hot
chocolate or other beverages can be
heated very quickly. Place 300 ml/
½ pint/1¼ cups milk in a microwaveproof jug and microwave on HIGH
for 2–2½ minutes. Whisk until frothy.

To Make Mulled Wine

1 Mix 750 ml/1¼ pints/3 cups red
wine, 12 cloves, 2 small cinnamon
sticks, the grated rind and juice of
1 large orange and 1 lemon, and
30-45ml/2-3 tbsp brown sugar in a
microwaveproof bowl or jug.

2 Microwave on HIGH for about
5 minutes, or until almost boiling. Add
extra sugar to taste, if liked, and serve
the wine warm. This serves about six.

Basic Recipes

The microwave is invaluable for cooking a range of basic recipes and sauces in particular, because they complement so many dishes.

Hollandaise Sauce

1 Place 115 g/4 oz/½ cup butter in a large microwaveproof jug and microwave on HIGH for 1½ minutes until melted. Whisk in 45 ml/3 tbsp lemon juice, 2 egg yolks, a pinch of mustard powder and salt and pepper to taste.

2 Microwave on MEDIUM for 1 minute, whisk and serve. This sauce is delicious with poached salmon or cooked asparagus. Serves 4–6.

White Pouring Sauce

1 Place 25 g/1 oz/2 tbsp butter in a microwaveproof jug and microwave on HIGH for 30–60 seconds, until melted.

2 Stir in 25 g/1 oz/¼ cup plain flour and 300 ml/½ pint/1¼ cups milk. Microwave on HIGH for 3½–4 minutes, stirring or whisking once every minute, until smooth, boiling and thickened. Season to taste and serve. Makes 300 ml/½ pint/1¼ cups.

Variations

One-stage Sauce: place the flour and butter in a microwaveproof jug, then add the milk and whisk lightly. Microwave on HIGH as for step 2 of White Pouring Sauce.

Caper Sauce: add 15 ml/1 tbsp drained capers and 5 ml/1 tsp vinegar from the jar of capers or lemon juice to the cooked sauce. Good with cooked lamb.

Cheese Sauce: add 50–115 g/2–4 oz/½-1 cup grated cheese, a pinch of dry mustard powder and a pinch of cayenne pepper to the cooked sauce. Whisk or stir well. Serve with vegetables, eggs, fish or pasta.

Parsley Sauce: add 15–30 ml/ 1–2 tbsp chopped fresh parsley and a squeeze of lemon juice (optional) to the cooked sauce and whisk or stir well. Serve with fish, ham or bacon and vegetables.

Jacket Potatoes

1 Scrub and prick the potatoes. Place on a double thickness of kitchen paper. If cooking more than two potatoes, arrange them in a ring.

2 Microwave on HIGH for the time given, turning over halfway through. Leave to stand for 3–4 minutes.

3 The potatoes may be cut in half and the flesh forked up or mashed, then replaced in the shells, topped with cheese or butter and heated for a few seconds in the microwave to melt the butter or cheese before serving.

Cooking Times for Jacket Potatoes

1 x 175 g/6 oz potato	4–6 minutes
2 x 175 g/6 oz potatoes	6–8 minutes
3 x 175 g/6 oz potatoes	8–12 minutes
4 x 175 g/6 oz potatoes	12–15 minutes

Giblet Stock for Gravy

1 Place the giblets from a chicken, turkey or duck in a microwaveproof bowl with 300 ml/½ pint/1¼ cups boiling water and a few sliced seasoning vegetables, such as carrots, celery and onion.

2 Microwave the mixture on HIGH for 7–10 minutes. Strain and use the gravy as required.

Scrambled Eggs

Easy to do, and easy to wash up.

1 Place 15 g/½ oz/1 tbsp butter in a microwaveproof jug or bowl and microwave on HIGH for about 30 seconds to melt.

2 Beat 4 eggs with 30 ml/2 tbsp semi-skimmed or full cream milk and salt and freshly ground black pepper to taste. Add to the melted butter and microwave on HIGH for 1¼ minutes. Briefly stir or whisk the set pieces of egg from the outside of the bowl or jug to the centre.

3 Microwave on HIGH for a further 1¼–1¾ minutes, stirring or whisking twice. When about three-quarters cooked, there is still a significant amount of runny egg, as shown here. When they are cooked, the eggs are moist, not completely set. Leave to stand for 1–2 minutes, by which time the eggs will be set ready for serving. Serves 2.

Foods Not for the Microwave

The following foods, and methods of cooking, are not suitable for the microwave and they are best avoided.

Batter-based & Some Air-incorporated Recipes

Items such as Yorkshire pudding, soufflé, pancakes, choux pastry, batter-coated fish and whisked sponge mixtures need conventional cooking methods to become sufficiently crisp and firm. The microwave can be used, however, to make the basic sauce for a soufflé and will reheat cooked pancakes perfectly.

Meringues

These should be cooked in the conventional oven since they do not dry sufficiently and become crisp in the microwave.

Eggs in Shells

These are liable to explode owing to the build-up of pressure within the shell. Eggs can however be baked, scrambled, poached and "fried" in the microwave with superb results. The membrane surrounding a whole yolk should be pierced with the tip of a sharp knife.

Popcorn

This can prove to be too dry to attract microwave energy, although some manufacturers have produced microwave popcorn, sold in a special bag with seasonings and flavourings, and this works superbly. A special microwave popcorn machine can also be purchased to cook ordinary popcorn in the microwave.

Liquid in Bottles & Pots

Check that bottles do not have necks that are too narrow to allow sufficient steam to escape, as built-up pressure may cause them to shatter. Similarly, tall coffee pots with slim spouts can either break or cause the hot coffee to spurt out.

Deep-fat Frying

This is not recommended as it requires prolonged heating. It is also difficult to control the temperature of the fat and the food may burn.

Before You Begin

Getting used to the speed of microwave cooking does take time, patience and perseverance. The golden rule is to become a constant clock-watcher until you know your microwave really well. You will soon be able to cook the recipes in this book and, with growing confidence, adapt some of your own conventional favourites.

Microwave Powers & Settings

• All the recipes and the chart in this book were created and tested using microwave ovens with a maximum power output of 650–700 watts.

• The ovens had variable power and the descriptions used refer to the following power outputs.

• The microwave ovens used for testing had turntables – if yours does not and tends to have an irregular heating pattern with hot and cold spots, then follow the rules on turning, rotating and rearranging foods.

HIGH = 650–700 watts or 100%
MEDIUM
  HIGH = 500–550 watts or 75%

MEDIUM = 400 watts or 55–60%
LOW = 250 watts or 40%
DEFROST = 200 watts or 30%

The chart below gives the approximate power input in watts at the above levels and relative cooking times.

Guide to Comparative Microwave Oven Control Settings

Settings used in these recipes	Setting variations on popular microwave ovens	Approximate % power input	Approximate power outputs in watts	Cooking times in minutes – for times greater than 9 minutes simply add together the figures in the appropriate columns								
	1 keep warm **low**	2 25%	150W	4	8	12	16	20	24	28	32	36
Defrost	2 simmer **simmer**	3 30%	200W	3¼	6¾	10	13¼	16¾	20	23¼	26¾	30
Low	3 stew **medium/low**	4 40%	250W	2½	5	7½	10	12½	15	17½	20	22½
	4 defrost **medium**	5 50%	300W	2	4	6	8	10	12	14	16	18
Medium	5 bake **medium**	6 60%	400W	1¾	3¼	5	6¾	8¼	10	11¾	13¼	15
Medium High	6 roast **high**	7–8 75%	500–600W	1¼	2¾	4	5¼	6¾	8	9¼	10¾	12
High	7 full/high **normal**	10 100%	700W	1	2	3	4	5	6	7	8	9

Italian Fish Soup

Microwaves might have been invented for cooking fish, as the delicate texture of the flesh benefits from quick cooking.

Serves 4

INGREDIENTS
30 ml/2 tbsp olive oil
1 onion, thinly sliced
a few saffron threads
5 ml/1 tsp dried thyme
pinch of cayenne pepper
2 garlic cloves, finely chopped
2 x 400 g/14 oz cans tomatoes, drained
    and chopped
175 ml/6 fl oz/¾ cup dry white wine
1.85 litres/3¼ pints/8 cups
    hot fish stock
350 g/12 oz white fish fillets, skinned and
    cut into pieces
450 g/1 lb monkfish, cut
    into pieces
450 g/1 lb live mussels, scrubbed
    and debearded
225 g/8 oz prepared small squid,
    cut into rings
30 ml/2 tbsp chopped fresh parsley
salt and freshly ground
    black pepper
warm, crusty bread,
    to serve

1 Place the olive oil in a large microwaveproof bowl. Stir in the onion, saffron, thyme and cayenne pepper and season with salt to taste. Microwave on HIGH for 3 minutes, until soft. Add the garlic and then microwave on HIGH for 1 minute.

2 Stir in the tomatoes, wine and fish stock. Cover and microwave on HIGH for 10 minutes, stirring halfway through the cooking time.

3 Add the white fish fillet and monkfish pieces. Cover and microwave on HIGH for 2 minutes, stirring once.

4 Stir in the mussels and squid. Cover and microwave on HIGH for 2-3 minutes, stirring once. Stir in the parsley and season with salt and pepper to taste.

5 Ladle into warmed soup bowls and serve immediately with warm, crusty bread.

COOK'S TIP: Discard any mussels with broken shells and any that do not shut immediately when sharply tapped with the back of a knife. All the mussels should open during cooking. Discard any that remain closed.

Artichoke & Mushroom Soup

Serves 4

INGREDIENTS
30–60 ml/2–4 tbsp butter
115 g/4 oz/scant 2 cups sliced mushrooms
2 onions, chopped
450 g/1 lb Jerusalem artichokes, peeled and sliced
300 ml/½ pint/1¼ cups hot vegetable stock
300 ml/½ pint/1¼ cups milk
salt and freshly ground black pepper

1 Place the butter and mushrooms in a microwaveproof bowl. Cover and microwave on HIGH for 2 minutes. Using a slotted spoon, transfer the mushrooms to a plate. Add the onions and artichokes to the bowl. Cover and microwave on HIGH for 8 minutes, stirring halfway through cooking.

2 Add the vegetable stock to the bowl and microwave on HIGH for a further 5 minutes, until the artichokes are soft, then season to taste.

3 Process the soup in a blender or food processor, adding the milk slowly. Return to the bowl. Stir in the mushrooms. Microwave on HIGH for 2–3 minutes to reheat before serving.

Right: Artichoke & Mushroom Soup (top); Tomato & Red Pepper Soup

Tomato & Red Pepper Soup

Serves 4

INGREDIENTS
5 large tomatoes
30–60 ml/2–4 tbsp olive oil
1 onion, chopped
450 g/1 lb thinly sliced red peppers
30 ml/2 tbsp tomato purée
pinch of sugar
475 ml/16fl oz/2 cups hot vegetable stock
60 ml/4 tbsp soured cream (optional)
salt and freshly ground black pepper
chopped fresh dill, to garnish

1 Peel the tomatoes by plunging them into boiling water for 30 seconds. Chop the flesh and reserve any juice.

2 Place half the olive oil in a microwaveproof bowl with the onion. Microwave on HIGH for 2 minutes, stirring once. Add the peppers and the remaining oil, mixing well. Cover and microwave on HIGH for 5 minutes, stirring halfway through cooking.

3 Stir in the tomatoes, tomato purée, seasoning, sugar and a little stock. Cover and microwave on HIGH for 4 minutes, stirring halfway through.

4 Stir in the remaining stock and process. Season. Pour into bowls, swirl in the soured cream, if using, and garnish.

Chicken Liver & Marsala Pâté

This pâté is quick and simple to make, and has a delicious flavour.

Serves 4

INGREDIENTS
350 g/12 oz chicken livers, thawed
    if frozen
225 g/8 oz/1 cup butter, softened
2 garlic cloves, crushed
15 ml/1 tbsp Marsala
5 ml/1 tsp chopped fresh sage
salt and freshly ground
    black pepper
8 sage leaves, to garnish
thin toast, to serve

1 Trim any membranes and sinew from the livers, then rinse and pat dry with kitchen paper. Place 25 g/1 oz/ 2 tbsp of the butter in a microwave-proof bowl with the chicken livers and the garlic.

2 Cover loosely and microwave on HIGH for about 4 minutes, or until the livers are firm, but pink in the middle, stirring twice. Use a slotted spoon to transfer the livers to a blender or food processor. Add the Marsala and chopped sage.

3 Place 150 g/5 oz/10 tbsp of the butter in a microwaveproof bowl and microwave on HIGH for 1½ minutes to melt. Pour on to the livers and process until smooth. Season well.

4 Spoon the pâté into four individual pots and smooth the surface. Place the remaining butter in a microwaveproof bowl and microwave on HIGH for 1 minute to melt, then pour it over the pâtés. Garnish with sage leaves and chill until set. Serve with triangles of thin toast.

Eggs en Cocotte

A classic starter, these baked eggs are cooked on a base of ratatouille.

Serves 4

INGREDIENTS
4 eggs
20 ml/4 tsp freshly grated Parmesan cheese
chopped fresh parsley, to garnish

FOR THE RATATOUILLE
15 ml/1 tbsp olive oil
1 onion, finely chopped
1 garlic clove, crushed
2 courgettes, diced
1 small red pepper, seeded and diced
400 g/14 oz can chopped tomatoes with basil
salt and freshly ground black pepper

1 Place the oil in a microwaveproof bowl. Add the onion, garlic, courgettes and red pepper and microwave on HIGH for 3–4 minutes, stirring once, until softened.

2 Stir in the tomatoes, with salt and pepper to taste, and microwave on HIGH for 3–4 minutes, stirring once.

3 Divide the ratatouille among four individual microwaveproof dishes or large ramekins, each with a capacity of about 300 ml/½ pint/1¼ cups.

4 Make a small hollow in the centre of each portion of ratatouille and break in an egg.

5 Season each cocotte with freshly ground black pepper and sprinkle with the Parmesan cheese. Gently prick each yolk with a needle or wooden cocktail stick. Microwave on HIGH for 4–6 minutes, or until the eggs are just set. Sprinkle with fresh parsley and serve at once.

Tuna & Mixed Vegetable Pasta

Serves 4

INGREDIENTS
30 ml/2 tbsp olive oil
175 g/6 oz/2½ cups sliced button mushrooms
1 garlic clove, crushed
½ red pepper, seeded and chopped
15 ml/1 tbsp tomato purée
300 ml/½ pint/1¼ cups tomato juice
115 g/4 oz frozen peas
15–30 ml/1–2 tbsp drained pickled green
    peppercorns, crushed
275 g/10 oz/2½ cups dried pasta shapes
200 g/7 oz can tuna chunks in brine, drained
6 spring onions, sliced diagonally

1 Place the oil in a microwaveproof bowl with the mushrooms, garlic and red pepper. Cover and microwave on HIGH for 4 minutes, stirring halfway through cooking. Stir in the tomato purée, then add the tomato juice, peas and crushed peppercorns to taste. Cover the bowl and microwave on HIGH for a further 4 minutes, stirring halfway through cooking.

2 Bring a large saucepan of lightly salted water to the boil and cook the pasta for 10–12 minutes, until *al dente*. When the pasta is almost ready, add the tuna to the sauce and microwave on HIGH for 1 minute. Stir in the spring onions. Drain the pasta and tip into a warmed bowl. Pour over the sauce and toss to mix. Serve at once.

Sweet-&-sour Fish

Serves 4

INGREDIENTS
60 ml/4 tbsp cider vinegar
45 ml/3 tbsp light soy sauce
50 g/2 oz/¼ cup granulated sugar
15 ml/1 tbsp tomato purée
25 ml/5 tsp cornflour
250 ml/8 fl oz/1 cup water
1 green pepper, seeded and sliced
225 g/8 oz can pineapple pieces in fruit juice
225 g/8 oz tomatoes, peeled and chopped
225 g/8 oz/3¼ cups sliced button mushrooms
675 g/1½ lb chunky haddock fillets, skinned
salt and freshly ground black pepper

1 Mix the vinegar, soy sauce, sugar and tomato purée in a microwaveproof bowl. Blend the cornflour and water to a smooth paste with water, then add to the bowl, stirring well. Microwave on HIGH for 2–2½ minutes, stirring three times, until smooth, boiling and thickened.

2 Add the remaining ingredients, except the fish, to the sauce and microwave on HIGH for 2 minutes, stirring halfway through. Season to taste, then place the fish in a single layer in a shallow microwaveproof dish and pour over the sauce. Cover and microwave on HIGH for 8–10 minutes. Leave to stand for 5 minutes.

Right: Tuna & Mixed Vegetable Pasta (top); Sweet-&-sour Fish

Mediterranean Plaice

Sun-dried tomatoes, toasted pine nuts and anchovies make a flavoursome combination for the stuffing mixture.

Serves 4

INGREDIENTS
4 plaice fillets, about 225 g/8 oz
   each, skinned
75 g/3 oz/6 tbsp butter
1 small onion, chopped
1 celery stick, finely chopped
115 g/4 oz/2 cups fresh
   white breadcrumbs
45 ml/3 tbsp chopped
   fresh parsley
30 ml/2 tbsp pine nuts, toasted
3–4 pieces sun-dried tomatoes in oil,
   drained and chopped
50 g/2 oz can anchovy fillets, drained
   and chopped
75 ml/5 tbsp fish stock
freshly ground black pepper

1 Using a sharp knife, cut the plaice fillets in half lengthways to make eight smaller fillets.

2 Place the butter in a microwave-proof bowl and add the onion and celery. Cover and then microwave on HIGH for 2 minutes, stirring halfway through cooking.

3 Mix together the breadcrumbs, parsley, pine nuts, sun-dried tomatoes and anchovies. Stir in the softened vegetables with their buttery juices and season with pepper.

4 Divide the stuffing into eight portions. Taking one portion at a time, form the stuffing into balls, then roll up each one inside a plaice fillet. Secure the rolls with wooden cocktail sticks.

5 Place the rolled fillets in a buttered microwaveproof dish. Pour in the stock and cover the dish. Microwave on HIGH for 6–8 minutes, or until the fish flakes easily. Remove the cocktail sticks. Transfer the fish to a heated serving dish using a slotted spoon.

6 Sprinkle with a little extra parsley if you have it and then serve with a little of the cooking juices drizzled over.

Ginger Prawns

Serves 4

INGREDIENTS
225 g/8 oz raw tiger prawns, peeled
⅓ cucumber
15 ml/1 tbsp sunflower oil
15 ml/1 tbsp sesame seed oil
175 g/6 oz mangetouts, trimmed
4 spring onions, sliced diagonally
chopped fresh coriander, to garnish

FOR THE MARINADE
15 ml/1 tbsp clear honey
15 ml/1 tbsp light soy sauce
15 ml/1 tbsp dry sherry
2 garlic cloves, crushed
small piece of fresh root ginger, chopped
juice of 1 lime

1 Combine the marinade ingredients, stir in the prawns and marinate for 1–2 hours. Slice the cucumber in half lengthways, scoop out the seeds, then slice each half into crescents. Set aside.

2 Place the oils in a large microwave-proof bowl. Microwave on HIGH for 30 seconds. Drain the prawns (reserving the marinade) and add them to the oils. Cover and microwave on HIGH for 1½–2½ minutes, stirring halfway through cooking, until they begin to turn pink.

3 Add the mangetouts, cucumber and marinade, cover and microwave on HIGH for 1–2 minutes, stirring once. Stir in the spring onions and serve, sprinkled with coriander.

Provençal Fish

Serves 4

INGREDIENTS
4 white fish cutlets, about 150 g/5 oz each
45 ml/3 tbsp fish stock
45 ml/3 tbsp dry white wine
1 bay leaf, a few black peppercorns and a
    strip of pared lemon rind, for flavouring
sprigs fresh parsley, to garnish

FOR THE TOMATO SAUCE
400 g/14 oz can chopped tomatoes
1 garlic clove, crushed
15 ml/1 tbsp sun-dried tomato paste
15 ml/1 tbsp pastis
15 ml/1 tbsp drained capers
12–16 black olives, stoned
salt and freshly ground black pepper

1 Place all the tomato sauce ingredients in a microwaveproof bowl. Cover and microwave on HIGH for 4–6 minutes, stirring twice.

2 Place the white fish cutlets in a microwaveproof dish, pour over the stock and wine and add all the flavourings. Cover and microwave on HIGH for 5 minutes, rotating the dish twice. Leave to stand for 2 minutes.

3 Using a slotted spoon, transfer the fish to a heated dish. Strain the stock into the tomato sauce and mix well. Season the sauce, pour it over the fish and serve, garnished with parsley.

Right: Ginger Prawns (top); Provençal Fish

Hot Chilli Chicken

Serves 4

INGREDIENTS
30 ml/2 tbsp tomato purée
2 garlic cloves, roughly chopped
2 fresh green chillies, roughly chopped
5 dried red chillies
2.5 ml/½ tsp salt
1.5 ml/¼ tsp sugar
5 ml/1 tsp chilli powder
2.5 ml/½ tsp paprika
15 ml/1 tbsp curry paste
30 ml/2 tbsp oil
2.5 ml/½ tsp cumin seeds
1 onion, finely chopped
2 bay leaves
5 ml/1 tsp ground coriander
5 ml/1 tsp ground cumin
1.5 ml/¼ tsp ground turmeric
400 g/14 oz can chopped tomatoes
8 chicken thighs, skinned
5 ml/1 tsp garam masala
sliced fresh green chillies, to garnish
chappatis and natural yogurt, to serve

1 Process the tomato purée, garlic, green and dried red chillies, salt, sugar, chilli powder, paprika and curry paste to a smooth paste in a food processor or blender.

2 Place the oil in a large microwave-proof bowl and add the cumin seeds. Microwave on HIGH for 1½ minutes. Add the onion and bay leaves, cover and microwave on HIGH for 3 minutes.

3 Stir in the chilli paste. Cover and microwave on HIGH for 1½ minutes, then mix in the remaining ground spices, chopped tomatoes and 150 ml/ ¼ pint/⅔ cup water. Cover and microwave on HIGH for 3 minutes.

4 Add the chicken and garam masala. Cover and microwave on HIGH for 18–22 minutes, stirring twice, until the chicken is tender. Garnish with chillies and serve with chappatis and yogurt.

Beef & Mushroom Burgers

It's worth making your own burgers for the superior flavour.

Serves 4

INGREDIENTS
1 small onion, chopped
150 g/5 oz/2 cups small cup mushrooms
450 g/1 lb/4 cups lean minced beef
50 g/2 oz/1 cup fresh wholemeal breadcrumbs
5 ml/1 tsp dried mixed herbs
15 ml/1 tbsp tomato purée
plain flour, for shaping
salt and freshly ground black pepper
relish, lettuce, cherry tomatoes and burger
    buns or pitta bread, to serve

1 Process the onion and mushrooms in a food processor until finely chopped. Add the beef, breadcrumbs, herbs, tomato purée and seasoning. Process for a few seconds, until the mixture binds together but still has some texture.

2 Divide the mixture into four, then press into burger shapes with lightly floured hands.

3 To cook, place the burgers on a microwaveproof roasting rack and microwave, uncovered, for 6–7 minutes, turning over once. Leave to stand for 2–3 minutes. Alternatively, for a browner and crisper result, preheat a microwave browning dish according to the manufacturer's instructions. Add the burgers, pressing down well on to the base and microwave on HIGH for 5–5½ minutes, turning once. Leave to stand for 2–3 minutes.

4 Serve the burgers with relish, lettuce and cherry tomatoes, in burger buns or pitta bread.

Glazed Rack of Lamb

Bunches of redcurrants tied with chives provide a strong colour contrast.

Serves 4–6

INGREDIENTS
45 ml/3 tbsp redcurrant jelly
5 ml/1 tsp wholegrain mustard
2 best ends of lamb, each with 6 chops,
    trimmed of all fat
120 ml/4 fl oz/½ cup red wine
120 ml/4 fl oz/½ cup stock or water
salt and freshly ground black pepper
4–6 chives, wilted and 8–12 small bunches
    of redcurrants, to garnish

1 Place the jelly and mustard in a small microwaveproof bowl and microwave on HIGH for 1–2 minutes, stirring once, until the jelly is melted.

2 Brush the glaze over the lamb. Place the racks of lamb on a microwave roasting rack or upturned saucer in a microwaveproof shallow dish.

3 Microwave the lamb on HIGH for 18–22 minutes, or until cooked to your taste, rotating the dish and basting four times. Transfer the lamb to a warm platter, loosely cover it with foil and let it rest for 10 minutes.

4 Drain the fat from the roasting dish, leaving the sediment behind. Stir in the red wine and microwave on HIGH for 2–3 minutes.

5 Add the stock or water. Microwave on HIGH for 3–4 minutes, until reduced and slightly syrupy. Season, strain into a sauceboat and keep hot.

6 Wrap the chives around the redcurrant stems and tie in a neat knot. Carve the lamb into cutlets, spoon over a little of the sauce and garnish with the redcurrant bunches.

Chilli Con Carne

Serves 4

INGREDIENTS
15 ml/1 tbsp oil
225 g/8 oz/2 cups minced beef
1 onion, quartered
5 ml/1 tsp chilli powder
30 ml/2 tbsp plain flour
30 ml/2 tbsp tomato purée
150 ml/¼ pint/⅔ cup
    beef stock
200 g/7 oz can chopped tomatoes
200 g/7 oz can kidney beans,
    drained and rinsed
1 green pepper, seeded
    and chopped
15 ml/1 tbsp Worcestershire sauce
75 g/3 oz/½ cup long
    grain rice
salt and freshly ground
    black pepper
soured cream and chopped fresh
    parsley, to garnish

1 Place the oil, minced beef, onion and chilli powder in a microwaveproof bowl and microwave on HIGH for 6–8 minutes, stirring twice. Add the flour and tomato purée and microwave on HIGH for 30 seconds (stir once).

2 Stir in the stock and tomatoes, cover and microwave on HIGH for 12–15 minutes, stirring once. Mix in the beans, green pepper and sauce. Cover and microwave on HIGH for 5–7 minutes, stirring once.

3 Place the rice in a large microwave-proof bowl. Add 250 ml/8 fl oz/1 cup boiling water and a pinch of salt. Cover loosely and microwave on HIGH for 3 minutes. Stir, re-cover and microwave on MEDIUM for 12 minutes. Leave to stand, covered, for 5 minutes. Serve with the chilli con carne, garnished with soured cream and parsley.

Curried Lamb

Serves 4

INGREDIENTS
8 lean, boneless lamb leg steaks,
    about 500 g/1¼ lb total weight
1 onion, chopped
2 carrots, diced
1 celery stick, chopped
15 ml/1 tbsp hot curry paste
30 ml/2 tbsp tomato purée
475 ml/16 fl oz/2 cups stock
175 g/6 oz/1 cup green lentils
salt and freshly ground black pepper
fresh coriander leaves, to garnish
boiled rice and poppadums, to serve

1 Preheat a large browning dish, add the lamb steaks, pressing them down well on the dish and microwave on HIGH for 7–8 minutes, turning over halfway through cooking. If cooked on a microwaveproof plate, they will not brown in the same way.

2 Place the onion, carrots and celery in a microwaveproof casserole. Cover and microwave on HIGH for 4 minutes, stirring once. Stir in the curry paste, tomato purée, stock and lentils. Cover and microwave on HIGH for 10–15 minutes, or until the lentils are almost cooked. Add the steaks, cover and microwave on HIGH for 5–10 minutes, until tender. Season to taste, sprinkle with coriander and serve with rice and poppadums.

Right: Curried Lamb (top);
Pork Casserole

Pork Casserole

Serves 4

INGREDIENTS
4 lean pork loin chops
1 onion, thinly sliced
2 yellow peppers, seeded and sliced
10 ml/2 tsp medium-hot
    curry powder
15 ml/1 tbsp plain flour
250 ml/8 fl oz/1 cup chicken stock
115 g/4 oz/½ cup ready-to-eat
    dried apricots
30 ml/2 tbsp wholegrain mustard
salt and freshly ground black pepper
new potatoes or rice, to serve

1 Preheat a large browning dish. Trim the rind and fat off the pork chops. Place them in the browning dish, pressing them down well, and microwave on HIGH for 5–6 minutes, turning halfway through cooking. If cooked on a microwaveproof plate, they will not brown in the same way.

3 Place the sliced onion and yellow peppers in a microwaveproof casserole. Cover and microwave on HIGH for 4 minutes, stirring once. Stir in the curry powder and flour.

4 Stir in the stock, then add the apricots, mustard and pork chops. Cover and microwave on HIGH for 8–10 minutes, stirring once. Leave to stand, covered, for 10 minutes. Adjust the seasoning and serve hot, with new potatoes or rice.

Sweet Vegetable Couscous

A wonderful combination of sweet vegetables and spices, this makes a substantial midweek winter dish.

Serves 4–6

INGREDIENTS
pinch of saffron threads
45 ml/3 tbsp boiling water
15 ml/1 tbsp olive oil
1 red onion, sliced
2 garlic cloves, crushed
1–2 fresh red chillies, seeded and
    finely chopped
2.5 ml/½ tsp ground ginger
2.5 ml/½ tsp ground cinnamon
400 g/14 oz can chopped tomatoes
300 ml/½ pint/1¼ cups hot vegetable
    stock or water
4 carrots, cut into 5 mm/¼ in slices
2 turnips, cut into 2 cm/¾ in cubes
450 g/1 lb sweet potatoes, cut into
    2 cm/¾ in cubes
75 g/3 oz/⅔ cup raisins
2 courgettes, cut into
    5 mm/¼ in slices
400 g/14 oz can chick-peas, drained
    and rinsed
45 ml/3 tbsp chopped fresh parsley
45 ml/3 tbsp chopped fresh
    coriander leaves
salt and freshly ground black pepper
450 g/1 lb quick-cook couscous

1 Sprinkle the saffron strands into the boiling water and then set aside for 5 minutes to infuse. This will extract the subtle flavour and the brilliant yellow-orange colour.

2 Place the olive oil in a large microwaveproof bowl. Add the onion, garlic and chillies. Microwave on HIGH for 2 minutes, stirring halfway through cooking.

3 Add the ground ginger and cinnamon and microwave on HIGH for 1 minute.

4 Stir in the tomatoes, stock or water, infused saffron and liquid, carrots, turnips, sweet potatoes and raisins. Cover and microwave on HIGH for 15 minutes, stirring twice during the cooking time.

5 Add the courgettes, chick-peas, chopped fresh parsley and coriander, cover and microwave on HIGH for 5–8 minutes, stirring once, until the vegetables are tender. Season to taste.

6 Meanwhile, prepare the couscous following the packet instructions and serve it with the vegetables.

Risotto with Asparagus

This melt-in-the-mouth dish is a wonderful treat when asparagus comes into season in the early summer.

Serves 4

INGREDIENTS
30 ml/2 tbsp olive oil
1 onion, finely chopped
2 garlic cloves, crushed
225 g/8 oz/generous 1 cup Italian
    risotto rice
1.5 litres/2½ pints/6¼ cups hot
    vegetable stock
150 ml/¼ pint/⅔ cup dry white wine
225 g/8 oz asparagus spears, cut into
    2.5 cm/1 in pieces
50 g/2 oz/¼ cup butter
45 ml/3 tbsp freshly grated
    Parmesan cheese
salt and freshly ground black pepper

1 Place the oil, onion and garlic in a large microwaveproof bowl. Cover and microwave on HIGH for 3 minutes, stirring once.

2 Add the rice, stock and wine. Cover and microwave on HIGH for 7 minutes, stirring once. Stir in the asparagus, cover and microwave on HIGH for a further 6 minutes, stirring once. Leave to stand, covered, for 10 minutes.

3 Stir the butter and Parmesan into the risotto, season to taste and serve at once with salt and freshly ground black pepper. Extra Parmesan can be handed round separately, if you like.

Tagliatelle with Courgettes

This scrumptious and satisfying pasta dish is quick and easy to prepare.

Serves 3–4

INGREDIENTS
5–6 ripe tomatoes
225 g/8 oz dried wholewheat
    tagliatelle
1.2 litres/2 pints/5 cups boiling water
30 ml/2 tbsp olive oil
1 onion, chopped
2 celery sticks, chopped
1 garlic clove, crushed
2 courgettes, sliced
30 ml/2 tbsp sun-dried tomato paste
salt and freshly ground black pepper
50 g/2 oz/½ cup flaked almonds, toasted,
    to serve

1 Place the tomatoes in a bowl and pour in boiling water to cover. After 30 seconds peel, then chop.

2 Place the tagliatelle in a large microwaveproof bowl with the boiling water. Microwave on HIGH for 6 minutes, stirring once. Leave to stand, covered, while cooking the sauce.

3 Place the oil in a microwaveproof bowl and add the onion, celery, garlic and courgettes. Cover and microwave on HIGH for 3–4 minutes, or until the onions are softened.

4 Stir in the tomatoes and sun-dried tomato paste. Microwave on HIGH for 3–4 minutes, then add salt and pepper.

5 Drain the pasta, return it to the bowl and add the sauce. Toss well. Transfer to a serving dish and scatter the toasted almonds over the top.

Cauliflower Cheese

Serves 4

INGREDIENTS
4 baby cauliflowers
120 ml/4 fl oz/½ cup water
250 ml/8 fl oz/1 cup single cream
75 g/3 oz dolcellate cheese, diced
75 g/3 oz Mozzarella cheese, diced
45 ml/3 tbsp freshly grated
   Parmesan cheese
freshly grated nutmeg
freshly ground black pepper
toasted breadcrumbs, to garnish

1 Place the cauliflowers floret-side down in a microwaveproof dish. Add the water, cover and microwave on HIGH for 9–11 minutes, rearranging once. Leave to stand for 3 minutes.

2 Place the cream in a small microwaveproof bowl with the cheeses. Microwave on HIGH for 2–3 minutes, stirring three times, until the cheeses have melted. Season with nutmeg and pepper.

3 Drain the cauliflowers thoroughly and place one on each of four warmed plates. Spoon a little of the cheese sauce over each cauliflower and sprinkle with toasted breadcrumbs. Serve at once.

Right: Cauliflower Cheese (top); Vegetable Hot-pot

Vegetable Hot-pot

Serves 4

INGREDIENTS
2 onions, sliced
4 carrots, sliced
1 small swede, sliced
2 parsnips, sliced
3 small turnips, sliced
½ celeriac, cut into matchstick strips
2 leeks, thinly sliced
1 garlic clove, chopped
1 bay leaf, crumbled
30 ml/2 tbsp chopped fresh mixed herbs,
   such as parsley and thyme
300 ml/½ pint/1¼ cups vegetable stock
15 ml/1 tbsp plain flour
675 g/1½ lb red-skinned potatoes, scrubbed
   and thinly sliced
50 g/2 oz/¼ cup butter
salt and freshly ground black pepper

1 Arrange all the vegetables, except the potatoes, in layers in a large microwaveproof dish with a tight-fitting lid. Season lightly and sprinkle with the garlic, bay leaf and herbs.

2 Blend the stock into the flour and pour over the vegetables. Arrange the potatoes in overlapping layers on top. Dot with butter and cover tightly. Microwave on HIGH for 10 minutes. Reduce to MEDIUM for 25–30 minutes, or until the vegetables are tender. Remove lid and cook under a preheated hot grill until golden. Serve hot.

Lemon & Ginger Spicy Beans

A quick meal, made with canned beans. You won't need extra salt, as canned beans tend to be salted.

Serves 4

INGREDIENTS
5 cm/2 in piece fresh ginger root,
    roughly chopped
3 garlic cloves, roughly chopped
250 ml/8 fl oz/1 cup
    cold water
15 ml/1 tbsp sunflower oil
1 large onion, thinly sliced
1 fresh red chilli, seeded and
    finely chopped
1.5 ml/¼ tsp cayenne pepper
10 ml/2 tsp ground cumin
5 ml/1 tsp ground coriander
2.5 ml/½ tsp ground turmeric
30 ml/2 tbsp lemon juice
75 g/3 oz/1½ cups chopped fresh
    coriander leaves
400 g/14 oz can black-eyed beans,
    drained and rinsed
400 g/14 oz can aduki beans, drained
    and rinsed
400 g/14 oz can haricot beans, drained
    and rinsed
freshly ground black pepper
crusty bread, to serve

COOK'S TIP: When selecting fresh
ginger choose a smooth plump root
and peel before use. Store and use
straight from the freezer, for grating.

1 Process the ginger, garlic and 60 ml/ 4 tbsp of the cold water in a blender or food processor until smooth.

2 Place the sunflower oil in a large microwaveproof bowl with the onion and chilli. Microwave on HIGH for 3 minutes, stirring halfway through the cooking time.

3 Add the cayenne pepper, cumin, ground coriander and turmeric, and microwave on HIGH for 1 minute. Stir in the ginger and garlic paste and microwave on HIGH for 1 minute.

4 Stir in the remaining water, lemon juice and fresh coriander. Cover and microwave on HIGH for 4 minutes.

5 Add all the beans to the mixture in the bowl and stir well. Cover and microwave on HIGH for 4–6 minutes, stirring halfway through cooking. Season with pepper and serve with crusty bread.

Spring Vegetable Medley

A colourful, dazzling medley of fresh and sweet young vegetables.

Serves 4

INGREDIENTS
15 ml/1 tbsp groundnut oil
1 garlic clove, sliced
2.5 cm/1 in piece fresh ginger root,
    finely chopped
115 g/4 oz baby carrots
115 g/4 oz patty pan squash
115 g/4 oz baby sweetcorn
115 g/4 oz French beans
115 g/4 oz sugar snap peas
115 g/4 oz young asparagus, cut into
    7.5 cm/3 in pieces
8 spring onions, cut into 5 cm/2 in pieces
115 g/4 oz cherry tomatoes
juice of 2 limes
15 ml/1 tbsp clear honey
15 ml/1 tbsp soy sauce
5 ml/1 tsp sesame oil

1 Place the groundnut oil in a large microwaveproof bowl. Add the garlic and ginger, and microwave on HIGH for 30 seconds. Stir in the carrots, patty pan squash, sweetcorn and beans. Cover and microwave on HIGH for 5 minutes, stirring once.

2 Add the sugar snap peas, asparagus, spring onions and cherry tomatoes. Cover and microwave on HIGH for 3–4 minutes, stirring halfway through cooking.

3 Mix the lime juice, honey, soy sauce and sesame oil together and add to the bowl. Stir well, then cover again and microwave on HIGH for 1–2 minutes, or until the vegetables are just tender but still crisp.

Mixed Mushroom Ragout

These mushrooms can be served hot or cold and made in advance.

Serves 4

INGREDIENTS
1 small onion, finely chopped
1 garlic clove, crushed
5 ml/1 tsp coriander seeds, crushed
30 ml/2 tbsp red wine vinegar
15 ml/1 tbsp soy sauce
15 ml/1 tbsp dry sherry
10 ml/2 tsp tomato purée
10 ml/2 tsp soft light brown sugar
75 ml/5 tbsp hot vegetable stock
115 g/4 oz baby button mushrooms
115 g/4 oz chestnut mushrooms, quartered
115 g/4 oz oyster mushrooms, sliced
salt and freshly ground black pepper
fresh coriander sprigs, to garnish

1 Mix the onion, garlic, coriander, vinegar, soy sauce, sherry, tomato purée, sugar and stock in a large bowl.

2 Cover and microwave on HIGH for 3 minutes, stirring once. Uncover and microwave on HIGH for a further 2–3 minutes, or until the liquid has reduced by half.

3 Add the mushrooms, mixing well. Cover and microwave on HIGH for 3–4 minutes, stirring once, until tender. Remove the mushrooms with a slotted spoon to a warmed serving dish.

4 Microwave the juices on HIGH for 3–5 minutes, or until reduced to about 75 ml/5 tbsp. Season to taste with salt and pepper.

5 Allow to cool for 2–3 minutes, then pour over the mushrooms. Serve hot or well chilled, garnished with fresh coriander.

Fruity Brown Rice Salad

An Oriental-style dressing gives this colourful rice salad extra piquancy.

Serves 4–6

INGREDIENTS
4 spring onions
115 g/4 oz/⅔ cup long grain brown rice
300 ml/½ pint/1¼ cups boiling water
1 small red pepper, seeded and diced
200 g/7 oz can sweetcorn, drained
45 ml/3 tbsp sultanas
225 g/8 oz can pineapple pieces in
    fruit juice
15 ml/1 tbsp light soy sauce
15 ml/1 tbsp sunflower oil
15 ml/1 tbsp hazelnut oil
1 garlic clove, crushed
5 ml/1 tsp finely chopped fresh
    root ginger
salt and freshly ground black pepper

1 Slice the spring onions diagonally and set them aside for garnishing.

2 Place the brown rice in a large microwaveproof bowl with the boiling water and a little salt. Cover the bowl loosely and microwave on HIGH for 3 minutes. Reduce the power setting to MEDIUM and microwave for a further 25 minutes, stirring twice. Leave to stand, covered, for 5 minutes.

3 Tip the rice into a serving bowl and add the red pepper, sweetcorn and sultanas. Drain the canned pineapple pieces, reserving the juice, then toss them lightly into the rice mixture.

4 Pour the reserved juice into a clean screw-top jar. Add the soy sauce, oils, garlic and ginger. Season to taste, then shake well to combine. Pour the dressing over the salad and toss. Scatter the spring onions over the top.

Watercress & Potato Salad

This colourful, nutritious salad is an ideal way of making the most of new potatoes when they are in season.

Serves 4

INGREDIENTS

450 g/1 lb small new potatoes, unpeeled
45 ml/3 tbsp water
1 bunch of watercress
200 g/7 oz/1½ cups cherry tomatoes, halved
30 ml/2 tbsp pumpkin seeds
45 ml/3 tbsp low-fat fromage frais
15 ml/1 tbsp cider vinegar
5 ml/1 tsp brown sugar
salt
paprika

COOK'S TIP: If you are preparing this salad in advance, mix the dressing in the jar and set aside. Shake the dressing again and toss it into the salad just before serving.

1 Place the potatoes and water in a microwaveproof bowl. Cover and microwave on HIGH for 7–10 minutes, stirring halfway through cooking. Leave to stand, covered, for 3 minutes, then drain and leave to cool.

2 Toss the potatoes, watercress, tomatoes and pumpkin seeds together.

3 Place the fromage frais, vinegar, sugar, salt and paprika to taste in a screw-top jar and shake well to mix. Pour over the salad just before serving.

VARIATION: To make Spinach and Potato Salad, substitute about 225 g/8 oz fresh baby spinach leaves for the watercress.

Poached Pears in Red Wine

This is an especially attractive dessert, as the wine colours the pears red.

Serves 4

INGREDIENTS
300 ml/½ pint/1¼ cups red wine
75 g/3 oz/⅓ cup caster sugar
45 ml/3 tbsp clear honey
juice of ½ lemon
1 cinnamon stick
1 vanilla pod, split open lengthways
5 cm/2 in thinly pared strip of orange rind
1 clove
1 black peppercorn
4 firm, ripe pears
whipped cream or soured cream, to serve

1 Place the wine, sugar, honey, lemon juice, cinnamon, vanilla, orange rind, clove and peppercorn in a microwave-proof bowl that will hold the pears upright. Microwave on HIGH for 3–5 minutes, stirring three times.

2 Meanwhile, peel the pears, leaving their stems intact. Take a thin slice off the base of each pear so that it will stand neatly square and upright. Place the pears in the wine mixture, spooning it over them. Three-quarters cover the dish with clear film or a lid. Microwave on HIGH for 5–6 minutes, until the pears are just tender when pierced with the tip of a knife. Turn the pears twice during cooking.

3 Carefully transfer the pears to another bowl using a slotted spoon. Microwave the poaching liquid, uncovered, on HIGH for 15–17 minutes, to reduce by half. Cool. Strain the syrup over the pears and chill. Serve the pears in individual dishes and spoon over the syrup. Serve with whipped or soured cream.

Sticky Toffee Pudding

This satisfying and warming dessert will become a winter favourite.

Serves 6

INGREDIENTS
115 g/4 oz/1 cup walnuts, toasted
  and chopped
175 g/6 oz/¾ cup butter
175 g/5 oz/scant 1 cup soft brown sugar
60 ml/4 tbsp single cream
30 ml/2 tbsp lemon juice
2 eggs, beaten
115 g/4 oz/1 cup self-raising flour

1 Grease a 900 ml/1½ pint/3¾ cup microwaveproof pudding basin and add half the walnuts.

2 Mix 50 g/2 oz/¼ cup of the butter with 50 g/2 oz/4 tbsp of the sugar, the cream and 15 ml/1 tbsp of the lemon juice in a small microwaveproof bowl.

3 Microwave on HIGH for 1½–2 minutes, stirring once, until smooth. Pour half into the pudding basin, then swirl to coat it a little way up the sides.

4 Beat the remaining butter and sugar until light. Gradually beat in the eggs. Fold in the flour, remaining nuts and lemon juice; spoon into the bowl. Three-quarters cover the basin with clear film and microwave on LOW for 7–10 minutes, until the mixture is well-risen and shrunk away from the sides of the bowl, but still wet on the surface. Leave to stand for 5 minutes.

5 Microwave the remaining sauce on HIGH for 1–1½ minutes to reheat. Unmould the pudding on to a warm plate and pour over the sauce.

Creole Bread & Butter Pudding

Sinfully rich and served with whisky-flavoured cream, this wonderful dessert is a long way from the traditional childhood pudding.

Serves 4–6

INGREDIENTS
4 ready-to-eat dried apricots,
　roughly chopped
15 ml/1 tbsp raisins
30 ml/2 tbsp sultanas
15 ml/1 tbsp chopped mixed peel
1 French loaf (about 200 g/7 oz),
　thinly sliced
50 g/2 oz/4 tbsp butter, melted
450 ml/³⁄₄ pint/scant 2 cups milk
150 ml/¹⁄₄ pint/²⁄₃ cup double cream
115 g/4 oz/½ cup caster sugar
3 eggs
2.5 ml/½ tsp vanilla essence
30 ml/2 tbsp whisky

FOR THE CREAM
150 ml/¹⁄₄ pint/²⁄₃ cup
　double cream
30 ml/2 tbsp Greek-style yogurt
15–30 ml/1–2 tbsp whisky
15 ml/1 tbsp caster sugar

1 Lightly butter a deep 1.5–1.75 litre/ 2½–3 pint/6¼–7½ cup microwave-proof dish that is suitable for grilling. Mix the apricots, raisins, sultanas and mixed peel, and sprinkle a little over the base of the dish. Brush both sides of the bread slices with melted butter.

2 Fill the dish with alternate layers of bread and dried fruit, finishing with a layer of bread.

3 Pour the milk and cream into a microwaveproof jug and microwave on HIGH for 3–4 minutes, or until just boiling. Meanwhile, whisk the sugar, eggs and vanilla essence together.

4 Whisk the hot milk and cream into the eggs and then strain the mixture over the bread and fruit. Sprinkle the whisky over the top. Press the bread into the milk and egg mixture, cover and leave to stand for at least 20 minutes.

5 Microwave on MEDIUM for 10–15 minutes, or until the mixture is almost set in the middle, rotating the dish four times during cooking. Place under a preheated hot grill until golden and crisp, if liked.

6 Just before serving, mix the cream, yogurt, whisky and sugar into a small microwaveproof bowl and microwave on HIGH for 1–2 minutes, stirring once. Serve with the hot pudding.

VARIATIONS: Try using chopped dates instead of apricots. Or sprinkle freshly grated or ground nutmeg between the layers for an extra spicy flavour.

Strawberry & Hazelnut Roulade

Light-as-air, this dreamy dessert looks pretty and tastes simply wonderful, yet it is quite simple to make.

Serves 6–8

INGREDIENTS
2 large eggs
50 g/2 oz/¼ cup caster sugar
50 g/2 oz/½ cup plain flour, sifted twice
40 g/1½ oz shelled hazelnuts, ground
120 ml/4 fl oz/½ cup double cream
1 egg white
175 g/6 oz/1½ cups sliced strawberries

1 Line a 28 x 18 cm/11 x 7 in shallow rectangular microwaveproof dish with lightly oiled greaseproof paper, leaving about 5 cm/2 in of the paper overlapping at the edges.

2 Whisk the eggs and caster sugar in a bowl until the mixture is very thick and has trebled in volume. Sift the flour over the egg mixture and fold it in with a metal spoon. Pour the mixture into the prepared dish, spreading it evenly.

3 Microwave the mixture on HIGH for 2½–3 minutes, until it is just firm in the centre, giving the dish a half turn once during the cooking time. Leave to stand for 3 minutes.

4 Sprinkle a sheet of greaseproof paper with the ground hazelnuts. Turn the sponge out on to the hazelnuts. Remove the lining paper.

5 Hold another piece of greaseproof paper under a tap for a few seconds to dampen it; crumple it up, spread it out again and lay it on top of the cooked sponge. Roll the cake up from one of the shorter edges, enclosing the paper. Let the cake cool completely on a wire rack.

6 Meanwhile, whip the cream until it stands in soft peaks. In another bowl, beat the egg white until stiff and fold into the cream, mixing well.

COOK'S TIP: Choose firm strawberries and slice them vertically down the centre. This will give a nice heart shape and attractive slices for decoration.

7 Unroll the sponge, remove the paper, spread the cream over the surface and dot with strawberries, reserving some for decoration. Roll up again and place on a serving plate, seam-side down. Chill for at least 1 hour, until firm enough to slice. Just before serving, trim the ends and decorate with strawberries.

Courgette & Walnut Loaf

Cardamom seeds impart their distinctive aroma to this loaf. Serve spread with ricotta and honey for a delicious snack.

Makes 1 loaf

INGREDIENTS
3 eggs
75 g/3 oz/⅓ cup light
  muscovado sugar
120 ml/4 fl oz/½ cup sunflower oil
225 g/8 oz/2 cups wholemeal flour
5 ml/1 tsp baking powder
5 ml/1 tsp bicarbonate of soda
5 ml/1 tsp ground cinnamon
3 ml/¾ tsp ground allspice
7.5 ml/1½ tsp green cardamoms, seeds
  removed and crushed
150 g/5 oz courgette,
  coarsely grated
115 g/4 oz/1 cup chopped walnuts
50 g/2 oz/¼ cup sunflower seeds

1 Line the base and sides of a 900 g/ 2 lb microwaveproof loaf dish with non-stick baking paper.

2 Beat the eggs and sugar together in a large bowl and gradually add the sunflower oil.

3 Sift the flour into a separate bowl, adding the baking powder, bicarbonate of soda, cinnamon and allspice.

4 Mix the dry ingredients into the egg mixture, adding the cardamoms, courgette and walnuts. Reserve 15 ml/ 1 tbsp of the sunflower seeds, then add the rest to the mixture.

5 Spoon the mixture into the loaf dish, level the top and sprinkle with the reserved sunflower seeds.

6 Shield each end of the dish with a smooth piece of foil, shiny side in. Cover with clear film and microwave on HIGH for 8–9 minutes, giving the dish a quarter turn three or four times.

7 Remove the clear film and foil for the last 1½ minutes, until the loaf is cooked, when a skewer inserted in the centre comes out clean. Allow to cool for 5 minutes before turning out on to a rack to cool. To colour the top brown under a preheated hot grill before serving, if you wish.

COMBINATION MICROWAVE: This recipe is suitable for cooking in a combination microwave. Follow the oven manufacturer's timing guide for good results.

Brown Soda Bread

Nothing tastes so good as home-made bread and this speedy recipe is simplicity itself. Make it and eat it on the same day.

Makes two 450 g/
1 lb loaves

INGREDIENTS
450 g/1 lb/4 cups plain flour
450 g/1 lb/4 cups wholemeal flour, plus
    extra for sprinkling
10 ml/2 tsp salt
15 ml/1 tbsp bicarbonate of soda
20 ml/4 tsp cream of tartar
10 ml/2 tsp caster sugar
50 g/2 oz/¼ cup butter
900 ml/1½ pints/3¾ cups buttermilk or
    skimmed milk

1 Sift all the dry ingredients into a large bowl, tipping any bran from the flour that remains in the sieve back into the bowl.

2 Rub the butter into the flour mixture, then add enough buttermilk or milk to make a soft dough. You may not need all of it, so add it cautiously.

3 Knead the dough lightly until smooth, then divide and shape it into two large rounds and place on lightly oiled plates. Make a deep cross in the top of each loaf. Sprinkle over a little extra wholemeal flour.

4 Cook each loaf separately. Microwave on MEDIUM for 5 minutes, give the plate a half turn and microwave on HIGH for a further 3 minutes. Brown the top under a preheated grill if liked. Allow to stand for 10 minutes, then transfer to a wire rack to cool.

Spiced Banana Muffins

Wholemeal muffins, with banana for added fibre, make a delicious, healthy treat at any time of the day, especially eaten with marmalade or jam.

Makes 12

INGREDIENTS
75 g/3 oz/⅔ cup wholemeal flour
50 g/2 oz/½ cup plain flour
10 ml/2 tsp baking powder
pinch of salt
5 ml/1 tsp mixed spice
40 g/1½ oz/¼ cup soft light brown sugar
50 g/2 oz/¼ cup soft margarine
1 egg, beaten
150 ml/¼ pint/⅔ cup semi-skimmed milk
grated rind of 1 orange
1 ripe banana
20 g/¾ oz/¼ cup porridge oats
20 g/¾ oz/scant ¼ cup chopped hazelnuts

1 Sift the dry ingredients into a bowl, then tip any bran from the flour into the bowl. Stir in the sugar.

2 Place the soft margarine in a microwaveproof bowl and microwave on HIGH for 1 minute, until melted. Cool the margarine slightly, then beat in the egg, milk and grated orange rind. Gently fold in the dry ingredients. Mash the banana, then stir it gently into the mixture; do not overmix.

3 Half-fill twelve double-thick bun cases. Cook six at a time, placing them in a microwaveproof muffin tray or in ramekin dishes. Mix the oats and nuts and sprinkle over each muffin.

4 Place in the microwave, arranging the dishes in a ring pattern. Microwave on HIGH for 2½–3 minutes, turning once. Cook the remaining six muffins. Cool on a wire rack.

This edition is published by Southwater

Southwater is an imprint of
Anness Publishing Ltd
Hermes House
88–89 Blackfriars Road
London SE1 8HA
tel. 020 7401 2077
fax 020 7633 9499

Distributed in the UK by
The Manning Partnership
251–253 London Road East
Batheaston
Bath BA1 7RL
tel. 01225 852 727
fax 01225 852 852

Distributed in the USA by
Anness Publishing Inc.
27 West 20th Street
Suite 504
New York
NY 10011
fax 212 807 6813

Distributed in Australia by
Sandstone Publishing
Unit 1, 360 Norton Street
Leichhardt
New South Wales 2040
tel. 02 9560 7888
fax 02 9560 7488

© 2001 Anness Publishing Limited

1 3 5 7 9 10 8 6 4 2

Publisher: Joanna Lorenz
Managing Editor: Helen Sudell
Editor: Valerie Ferguson
Series Designer: Bobbie Colgate Stone
Designer: Andrew Heath
Production Controller: Joanna King

Recipes contributed by: Catherine Atkinson,
Carol Bowen, Janet Brinkworth, Carla Capalbo,
Roz Denny, Christine France, Sarah Gates,
Shirley Gill, Judy Jackson, Manisha Kanani,
Annie Nichols, Maggie Pannell, Jenny Stacey,
Hilaire Walden, Laura Washington

Photography: Karl Adamson, Edward Allwright,
David Armstrong, Steve Baxter, James Duncan,
Amanda Heywood, David Jordan,
Michael Michaels

Notes:
For all recipes, quantities are given in both metric
and imperial measures and, where appropriate,
measures are also given in standard cups
and spoons.
Follow one set, but not a mixture, because they
are not interchangeable.

Standard spoon and cup measures are level.

1 tsp = 5 ml   1 tbsp = 15 ml

1 cup = 250 ml/8 fl oz

Australian standard tablespoons are 20 ml.
Australian readers should use 3 tsp in place of
1 tbsp for measuring small quantities of gelatine,
cornflour, salt etc.

Medium eggs are used unless otherwise stated.